ROY OF THE ROVERS FOOTBALL QUIZ BOOK 1979-1980

ROY OF THE ROVERS

FOOTBALL QUIZ BOOK 1979-1980

Edited by
Barrie J. Tomlinson

Introduction by
Trevor Francis

MIRROR BOOKS

© 1979 by Mirror Books Ltd.
First published in Great Britain in August 1979 by
Mirror Books Ltd., Athene House,
66/73 Shoe Lane, London EC4P 4AB
for Mirror Group Newspapers Ltd.
Printed and bound in Great Britain by
Cox & Wyman Ltd., Reading.

ISBN 0 85939 164 7

CONTENTS

INTRODUCTION

I often see myself referred to in the press as Britain's first million-pound footballer. How much would Roy of the Rovers cost, should he ever be available for transfer? How much would a club pay for a footballer who never ages? Ten million at least?

Seriously, it's a great honour for me to write the foreword to the second *Roy of the Rovers Football Quiz Book*. I note that Eric Morecambe did this task last year . . . no wonder Luton Town was mentioned so many times! However, there wasn't a section on Eric in last year's book, so I'm delighted to see that I've got two pages to myself in this book. Fame at last!

Like most of today's soccer stars, I was introduced to Roy of the Rovers at an early age, when I started reading Roy's adventures in the pages of *Tiger*. That magazine is still going strong (I should know, because I write a regular column for it) but now Roy stars in his own paper and I'm pleased that he's branching out, to produce books such as this.

Looking through the questions in this book, I can see that anyone getting a high proportion of correct answers can rightly claim to be a football expert. I'm certain that when my fellow professionals buy a copy of this quiz book, they'll spend many hours puzzling over the questions. We're always in need of something to pass the time when we're travelling to away matches . . . and this book is just the thing!

I remember occasions when I've been travelling to overseas matches with players and journalists, that the press people have often tested our soccer knowledge. With the *Roy of the Rovers Football Quiz Book 1979-1980*, I'll be able to get my own back, and see just what the football writers know. It should be interesting!

Soccer really is an international game these days and I think that is reflected in the questions in this book. Once upon a time, we only seemed to know about the players in our own country, but now more and more players from overseas are joining British clubs and our players are playing more matches abroad . . . sometimes for their own clubs and sometimes as 'guest' players for overseas teams.

My matches with Detroit Express have shown me a great deal of soccer in the United States and I was amazed by the number of British players that were playing in America and the way information about our game was publicised in the States. I'm sure that American soccer fans, for example, will be able to answer quite a lot of the questions set in this book.

I don't know if Roy of the Rovers plans to play for an American club (maybe I can fix it with Detroit Express!) but I do know he's just the right person to present a book like this. Football needs a good image and for twenty-five years, Roy's image has been the very best in soccer. He's always been a superb example to football fans of all ages and I'm certain this book will be a big hit with all age groups. Every football supporter likes to think of himself (or herself) as a soccer expert . . . by the time they've read this book they'll know for sure if they are or not. You'll find the answers at the back of the book . . . but no cheating, that's not the way Roy of the Rovers does things!

That's enough from me. It's time for you to put on your soccer thinking caps and see just what you do know. Good luck . . . it may be harder than you think!

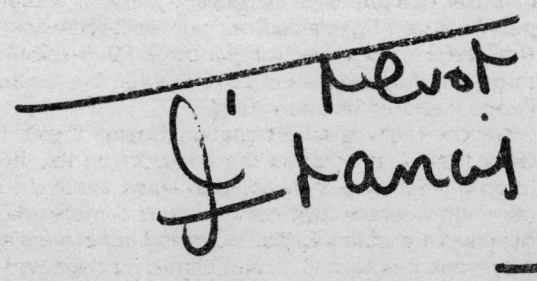

THE FIRST DIVISION

League football is the backbone of the game in the British Isles. In this ten-page section we test your knowledge of the Football League, from the biggest club to the smallest, from the most successful to the least successful.

1 When was the League founded?

2 Which club won it in the very first season?

3 Which club has Ayresome Park for its home ground?

4 Charlton Athletic's highest ever position in the First Division was in . . . 1936-7, 1938-9, 1947-8?

5 How many times have Leicester City won the First Division championship?

6 Liverpool won the First Division by eight points in 1978-9. But who was second?

7 Which club has won the First Division title more often, Derby County or Chelsea?

8 Name the three clubs relegated from the First Division in season 1977/8?

9 Only one team failed to win away in the First Division in 1978-9. Name them and their well-known manager.

10 Who are 'The Rams'?

start

Take one letter from each segment to spell the name of a
famous Southern club.

9

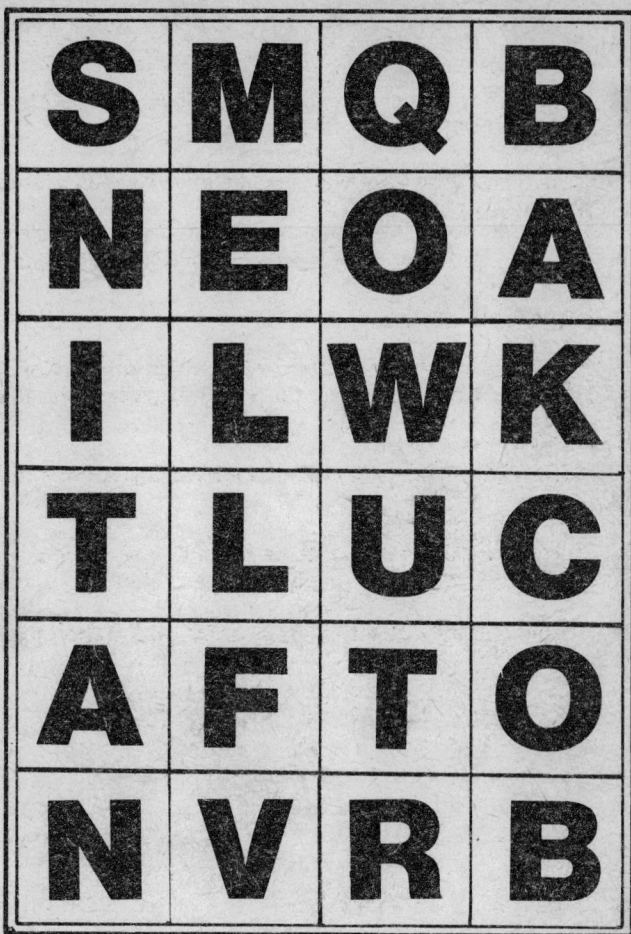

S	M	Q	B
N	E	O	A
I	L	W	K
T	L	U	C
A	F	T	O
N	V	R	B

Take one letter from each horizontal line to spell a First Division club.

1 Which club once played at the Blue House Field, Hendon?

2 Who won the First Division championship in 1953/4, 1957/8 and 1958/9?

3 Manchester City have won the title once, twice or three times in their history. Which?

4 Who succeeded Don Revie as manager of Leeds United?

5 Ipswich play at . . .?

6 Derby County have had two ex-Scottish international wing-halves as manager since the 1939-45 War. Who are they?

7 When did Coventry City reach the First Division for the first time?

8 The first Chelsea manager to be appointed after the War who wasn't a former Chelsea player was . . . ?

9 Carlisle had one season in the First Division. When was it?

10 What is the name of the Carlisle ground?

THE SECOND DIVISION

1 Fulham won the Second Division championship in . . . ?

2 Which club once played at The Nest?

3 Have Colchester United ever played in the Second Division?

4 Oldham Athletic are known as The . . . ?

5 Which Argentinian player joined a Second Division club before the 1978-9 season—and later found himself relegated?

6 Which club were unbeaten at home for 59 matches between 1964/7?

7 The player who holds West Ham's League appearance record is . . . ?

8 Watford are back in the Second Division. When were they relegated?

9 Which club won the Second Division championship in 1974/5?

10 Who was the Second Division's leading scorer in 1973/4?

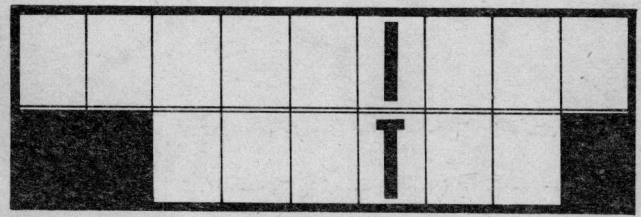

First elected to the Second Division in 1892, this club have been in and out of it ever since. Can you fill in the missing blanks?

THE THIRD
DIVISION

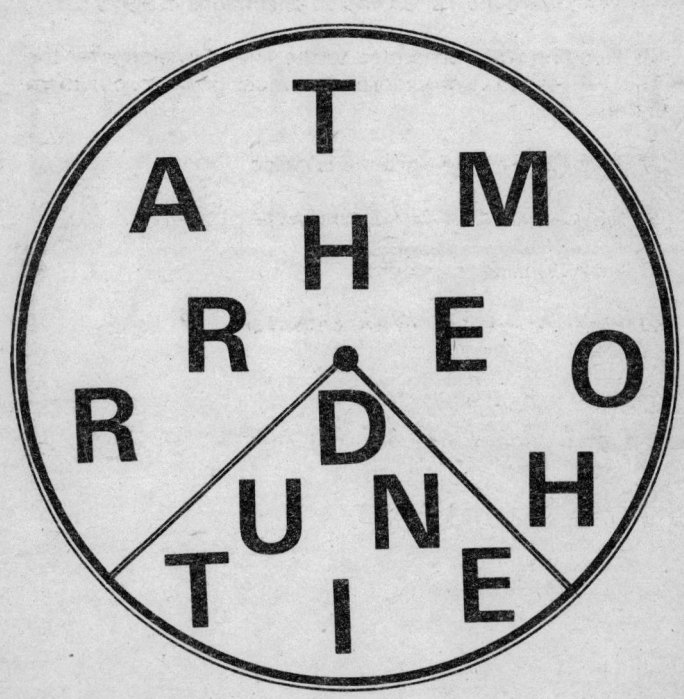

Rearrange the letters and you will find a Third Division club from the North.

1 When were QPR last in the Third Division?

2 Which club plays at Gigg Lane?

3 John Docherty's predecessor as manager of Cambridge United was . . . ?

4 Have Tottenham Hotspur ever played in the Third Division?

5 Who were the Third Division champions in 1972/3?

6 Reading were promoted to the Third Division after the 1978-9 season. Who scored the most goals to put them there?

7 Gillingham's home ground is called . . . ?

8 Which club is known as The Bees?

9 Name Chester's colours.

10 Sheffield Wednesday are known as . . . ?

THE FOURTH DIVISION

1 Name the club that were losing finalists in the 1961-2 League Cup Final?

2 Doncaster Rovers have the biggest pitch in the Football League. True or false?

3 The club that has had to re-apply for election to the Fourth Division more often than any other is . . .?

4 Which club lost its League status to Wigan in 1978?

5 During Oxford's early success in the Fourth Division, after their election in 1962, two brothers masterminded most of their victories. Who were they?

6 When did the Fourth Division begin?

7 In 1975-6 and 1977-8, the same manager achieved promotion from the Fourth Division with different clubs. Who was he?

8 Which Fourth Division club is known as The Hatters?

9 Which Fourth Division club has the inscription "Upon this Rock" in its club badge?

10 Newport County are known as The Ironsides. True or false?

PROGRESS WITH UNITY

This is the badge of a well-known but relatively new, Fourth Division club. Name the club.

SCOTLAND

Talk of devolution hasn't affected Scottish football. The Scots have always been apart in producing players of great natural ability even if the standards of their club football may have declined in recent years. These questions are about some of the leading Scots players.

1 One of the hardest midfield players in his generation. Played 31 times for Scotland 1951-65 and his clubs were Celtic and Leeds. Name him.

2 Bertie Auld (Celtic) played once, twice or three times for his country?

3 Billy Liddell played for a Mersey club. Was it Everton or Liverpool?

4 Lou Macari first played for Scotland as a substitute against Wales in 1972. True or false?

5 Who had more caps, Ian St. John or Billy Steel?

6 Which club did John White play for before signing for Spurs?

7 The most capped Scottish centre-half was . . .?

8 Name the player who holds the Scottish League all-time scoring record.

9 Which manager played more times for his country— Billy McNeil of Celtic or John Greig of Rangers?

10 Did Bill Shankly ever play for Scotland?

This player holds the Scottish record for the highest number of caps. Can you unjumble his name?

ROUGH
KENNEDY
BURNS
FORSYTH
BUCHAN
RIOCH
MASSON
HARTFORD
DALGLISH
JORDAN
JOHNSTON

Substitutes:
GEMMILL
MACARI

This was a team which some people said brought disgrace on Scottish football. What was the match?

1 Scotland had two points deducted from their total in Group 4 of the 1978 World Cup. Why?

2 Which Italian club signed Denis Law in 1961?

3 Scotland's first defeat at home against a foreign country was in 1950. Name the country.

4 Manchester United bought Law back from Italy for a then record fee in 1962. What was it?

5 A Scottish centre-forward has twice scored five goals in an international, in 1925 and 1929. He was Hughie . . .

6 Scotland first played Argentina in 1977. Was the score 1-1, 2-2 or 3-3?

7 Scotland's leading goalscorer in internationals is . . .?

8 Before he joined Manchester United, Martin Buchan was with . . .?

9 Everton goalkeeper George Wood's first club was East Stirling, Blackpool or Glasgow Rangers?

10 Has Bruce Rioch ever played for Luton?

WALES

Under Mike Smith, Welsh football has enjoyed a comeback in recent years. They are a small army but they've won some big battles.

1 The leading scorer for Wales in international football is . . . .

2 Who played the most games for Wales, Ivor Allchurch or John Charles?

3 Ray Mielczarek and Dick Krzywicki were Welsh internationals. True or false?

4 How many players have been capped by Wales whose surname is Williams? 6, 12 or 22?

5 Wrexham's appearance record is held by . . .?

6 Cardiff City were the only non-English club to win the F.A. Cup. In which year?

7 Cardiff are nicknamed 'The . . .'?

8 Have Swansea City ever played in the First Division?

9 When did Wales last win the Home International championship outright?

10 The oldest player ever to play for Wales was Billy M. . . . .

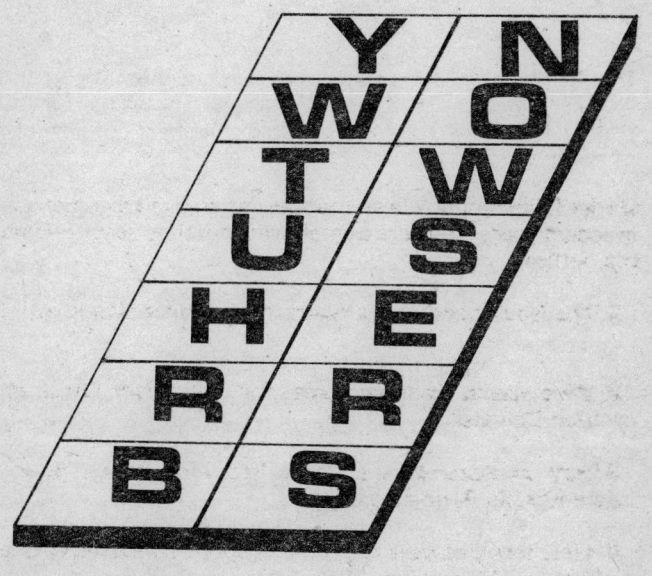

The Welsh Cup winners in 1979 are all muddled up in the square above!

NORTHERN IRELAND

Danny Blanchflower has added flair and humour to the Northern Irish scene in recent years. He knows he has few players to choose from but he makes the best possible use of them.

1 What year did Pat Jennings make his debut for Northern Ireland?

2 The Irish had two world famed wingers in post-war years, Billy Bingham and George Best. Which one has the most caps?

3 A former Irish national manager is now playing and working in the North American Soccer League. What is his name?

4 Name the Southampton defender who took over from Allan Hunter as Northern Ireland centre-half?

5 Harry Gregg managed three League clubs. What were they?

6 Ireland's first international was in 1882 and they lost 13-0 . . . to whom?

7 Who had more international appearances, Terry Neill or Danny Blanchflower?

8 Sammy McIlroy, David McCreery and Chris McGrath were all born in the same city. Name it.

9 When England beat Northern Ireland 4-0 in February, 1979 an England player scored twice. Who was he?

10 Name an Irish League side whose name begins with A.

K	C	I	R	R	A	C
S	R	E	G	N	A	R

An unfancied side that won the Irish Cup in 1976. Two words – the first beginning with 'C'.

THE WORLD CUP

The 1978 World Cup was the 11th since the competition started in Uruguay in 1930. There were fears that it would be dogged by disturbances and political troubles but it turned out to be one of the most successful ever held. Here are some questions about the 1978 and earlier tournaments.

1 Who was the top scorer in 1978?

2 How many goals did he score?

3 Name the three players who were sent off.

4 . . . was the only unbeaten team.

5 Of the 14 penalties awarded, how many were converted? 10, 12 or 13?

6 Who scored Holland's goal in the Final?

7 The referee was Italian. He was S. G. . . . .

8 The first goal of the tournament was scored by whom?

9 What was the score in the third place match?

10 The Brazilian goalkeeper equalled the Goals Conceded record of 3 which was previously shared by Gordon Banks and Jan Jongbloed. What was his name?

Only two goals in the 1978 competition were scored direct from free kicks. Who scored them?

SOUTH AMERICA----------

EUROPE----------

In the 11 World Cup tournaments, how many times has a
South American country won and how many times has a
European country triumphed?

1 Name the three goalkeepers in the Scottish World Cup squad.

2 Three players from Nottingham Forest were in the squad. Who were they?

3 Which squad was Ronald Worm in?

4 And Erich Beer?

5 Osvaldo Ardiles and Rene Houseman were team mates at which club?

6 The manager of the Holland side was Ernst H . . . .

7 Name the first choice Swedish goalkeeper.

8 Dutch forward Johnny Rep was playing for which French club at the time?

9 Who scored Scotland's goal in the 3–1 defeat by Peru?

10 In Holland's 2–1 victory over Italy the same player scored for both sides. What was his name?

	P.	W.	D.	L.	F.	A.	Pts.
Italy	6	5	0	1		4	10
England	6	5	0	1	15	4	10
Finland	6	2	0	4	11	16	4
Luxembourg	6	0	0	6	2	22	0

The vital figure which cost England a place in the 1978 Finals has been left out of the Group 2 qualifying table. Can you supply it?

1 Name the only country to have appeared in the final stages of all 11 World Cup tournaments.

2 The leading scorer in the 1970 tournament in Mexico was . . . with 10 goals.

3 Who scored from the penalty spot for Holland in their 2–1 defeat in the 1974 Final?

4 What was the score in the third place match in 1966?

5 Geoff Hurst scored a hat-trick in the 1966 Final but who scored the other goal in England's 4–2 victory over West Germany?

6 What was the score at half-time?

7 Who was the leading scorer in the 1966 tournament?

8 The most number of goals in a World Cup was 140 in 26 matches, or 5.3 per match in which year?

9 How many times have Scotland reached the Finals?

10 Pat Partridge, England's referee at the 1978 Finals, is a . . . in real life.

KEVIN KEEGAN
Europe's Footballer of the Year 1978

Only one English footballer has ever gone to play in Europe and become really successful – Kevin Keegan. This section is devoted to him.

1 Who came second in the 1978 European Footballer of the Year competition?

2 What is Kevin's nickname in Hamburg?

3 Where was Kevin born?

4 What was his first professional club?

5 In the 1975–6 season he played 41 out of Liverpool's 42 League games. Which number shirt did he wear?

6 When did Kevin sign for Hamburg SV?

7 And what was the fee?

8 Two months later Liverpool bought Kenny Dalglish as his replacement from Celtic. For how much?

9 Against whom did Kevin make his England debut?

10 And in what year?

1 Kevin was substituted against West Germany in Munich in February, 1978. Who took over?

2 In April, 1978, Kevin scored England's only goal against one of the leading South American countries at Wembley. What was the name of the country?

3 Kevin's goal tally for England is now in double figures. How many other players have scored 10 or more goals for England since the 1939-45 World War?

4 What year did Liverpool sign Kevin?

5 What was the fee?

6 Who recommended him to Liverpool?

7 Who was the Liverpool manager at the time?

8 How many goals did Kevin score in the 1974 F.A. Cup Final victory over Newcastle?

9 Who marked Kevin in the 1977 European Cup Final against Borussia Mönchengladbach?

10 In the 83rd minute of that match, Kevin was brought down and the resultant penalty was Liverpool's third goal. Who took it?

WINGERS

Wingers virtually disappeared during the Sixties but in recent years have slowly been coming back into the game. Here are some teasers about the wingers in our game.

1 Who played more times for England, Sir Stanley Matthews or Tom Finney?

2 Which one scored the most goals?

3 A winger who played all his career for Blackburn Rovers was one of England's highest post-war scorers with 11 goals. What was his name?

4 One of the few wingers to become a League club manager managed Southport, Plymouth Argyle, Linfield, Everton, Northern Ireland and Greece. What was his name?

5 Manchester United played with two wingers in the 1976 F.A. Cup Final. Name them.

6 Willie Johnston, the WBA winger, was signed in 1972 from which club?

7 Peter Taylor, the Tottenham Hotspur winger, was previously with which clubs?

8 Jimmy Neighbour is a winger with which First Division side?

9 The £165,000 QPR paid for Dave Thomas in 1972 was a club record at the time. Which club sold him?

10 John Chiedozie was born in . . .?

Can you identify this former Millwall and Manchester United winger?

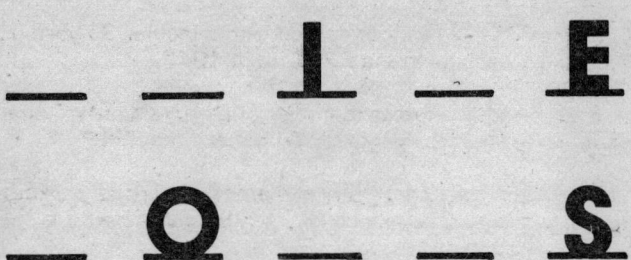

_ _ T _ _ E
_ O _ _ _ S

This is the player who was generally regarded as outstanding in the 1978 F.A. Cup Final between Arsenal and Ipswich Town.

1 Liverpool winger Steve Heighway was born in . . .?

2 Manchester City and England winger Peter Barnes had a famous father in football. What was his name?

3 Manchester United signed Steve Coppell from . . .?

4 Name the Argentinian winger Middlesbrough tried to buy in 1978.

5 This Chelsea winger scored a spectacular 35-yard goal against Liverpool in the F.A. Cup in 1978.

6 During his reign as manager of Derby County, Tommy Docherty sold two wingers. Who were they?

7 Fulham manager Bobby Campbell signed a famous winger from a Scottish club in 1979. Name him.

8 In the 1978–79 season, Leeds often used two international wingers, one from Wales and one from Scotland. Who were they?

9 A winger played a record number of games for Southampton. What was his name?

10 A famous winger scored 157 goals for Arsenal. He was Cliff . . . .

1 How many F.A. Cup winners medals did Stanley Matthews win?

2 Matthews started his League career in 1930, 1931 or 1935?

3 How many years did he play League football?

4 When was he knighted for services to football?

5 Where does he live now?

6 Tom Finney was Footballer of the Year in . . . .

7 Which famous Welsh winger was known as 'Old Skinny'?

8 Which Arsenal winger gained the most England caps?

9 Name three wingers on Tottenham's books during their Double Year. Cliff . . ., Terry . . ., Terry . . . .

10 This Scots winger was called 'the wee blue devil' He was Alan M . . . .

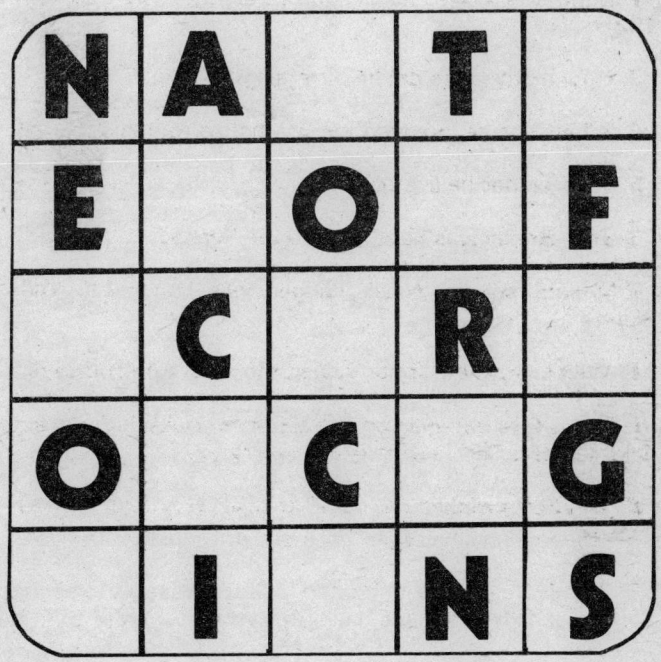

N	A		T	
E		O		F
	C		R	
O		C		G
	I		N	S

World-famed winger with Real Madrid in their European Cup winning days. There are 5 letters in his surname.

DEFENDERS

Defenders are the backbone of any side. The strikers get most of the glory but the men at the back have to do the hard bit and often it is an unglamorous role.

1 Only one player appeared in all 42 League matches for West Ham in the season 1977–78. Despite playing with his socks round his ankles, he was never injured enough to need a rest. Who is he?

2 A Southampton defender with an odd name is usually given the man to man marking assignments. Name him.

3 Name three Nottingham Forest back four defenders who have international caps.

4 Leeds centre-half Paul Hart was previously with . . .?

5 In March, 1979 a converted forward was sold to Leeds for a record fee for a full-back. Who was he?

6 Chelsea centre-half Mickey Droy was born near which First Division ground?

7 Coventry full-back Bobby McDonald was bought from . . .?

8 Crystal Palace centre-half Ian Evans had one of the worst broken legs of recent times. Who was the other player involved in the incident which led to his injury?

9 Name the son of a footballing father in Everton's defence.

10 Ipswich defender Russell Osman was once a rugby player. True or false?

Name this well-known North London publican! He used to play for Arsenal!

Ipswich Town's longest-serving player. Can you identify him?

1 Who is the taller of the Manchester City centre-backs, Tommy Booth or Dave Watson?

2 Who has more caps for Scotland, Martin Buchan or Gordon McQueen?

3 Brian Greenhoff was born in . . .?

4 Who was the defender QPR signed for Orient for £235,000 in 1978?

5 Stoke City centre-half Dennis Smith has played for two other League Clubs. True or false?

6 Two Wolverhampton central defenders. George . . . and Bob . . . .

7 Which were the previous clubs of Wrexham centre-half John Roberts?

8 Who was capped more times for England – Colin Todd or Norman Hunter?

9 West Ham full-back Frank Lampard has one England cap. In what year and against whom?

10 Which Scottish defender scored an 'own goal' in the 1–1 draw against Wales in May, 1978?

1 Billy Wright's 100th cap in 1959 was against . . .?

2 He went on to gain how many caps?

3 Manchester United and Eire centre-half Johnny Carey was once sacked as manager of a leading First Division club in a taxi. What was the name of the club?

4 Sir Alf Ramsey played 316 League matches between 1946–55. For which clubs?

5 One of England's greatest centre-halves was Neil Franklin. Did he play 27, 34 or 66 times for England?

6 Who marked Franz Beckenbauer in the 1966 World Cup Final?

7 Who won most caps for his country, Ray Wilson or George Cohen?

8 Bobby Moore was born where?

9 Who played more League matches, Bobby Charlton or Jack Charlton?

10 Juventus paid a world record fee for a Welsh defender in 1957. Who was he?

Ex-Liverpool centre-half called 'The Colossus' by his manager Bill Shankly. His Christian and Surname are jumbled in the segments.

F.A. CUP

The F.A. Cup remains the world's most exciting Cup competition with 250 million watching the Final every year on TV around the world. Most people think they are experts on the Cup. Are you?

1 The two clubs with most wins in finals at Wembley are . . . ?

2 How many post-war Finals have gone to extra time? Four, five or six?

3 When did Portsmouth win the Cup?

4 Have Notts County ever reached the Final?

5 Which club has won the Cup more often, Manchester City or Manchester United?

6 Hartlepool United beat Crystal Palace in the fifth round in 1978. Who knocked them out in the next round?

7 Who scored Sunderland's goal against Leeds in their 1–0 Cup Final triumph in 1973?

8 Roger Osborne was helped off the field after scoring for Ipswich against Arsenal in the 1978 Final. What was wrong with him?

9 Who was the goalkeeper who 'broke' his neck at Wembley?

10 Did Gordon Banks ever win a F.A. Cup-winners' medal?

Can you recognise this striker (left) who scored one of Manchester United's goals in the 1977 F.A. Cup Final?

Can you identify this famous forward who gained a winner's and a loser's F.A. Cup medal while with Arsenal?

1 Do the club managers lead the two teams on to the field at Wembley?

2 Arsenal have never been beaten by a non-League club. True or false?

3 The non-League club with most victories over League opposition is . . . Yeovil or Peterborough?

4 Who scored for Preston in the last minute of extra time in 1938?

5 When Stanley Matthews at last received his F.A. Cup Winner's medal in 1953, who presented it to him?

6 A Chelsea full-back let a header from Jack Charlton go through his legs in the 1970 Final. Who was he?

7 Who scored the first goal in a Wembley Final? David J . . . .

8 Who was the Cornishman who scored two goals for Everton in the 1966 Final?

10 Who's won the Cup the most times . . . Liverpool or Everton?

1 The first F.A. Cup Final was held in what year?

2 Where?

3 The highest number of fans to watch a Final was 126,047 in what year?

4 Who were the first winners?

5 The first winners after the Second World War in 1946 were . . .?

6 Charlton, team they defeated, won in 1947. Whom did they beat?

7 The 1948 Final went to extra time. True or false?

8 Newcastle United won the Cup in 1951 and 1952. Who were their opponents?

9 Who was Newcastle's captain? Joe . . . .

10 On neither occasion did they concede a goal. Who were their goalkeepers? Jack . . . and Ron . . . .

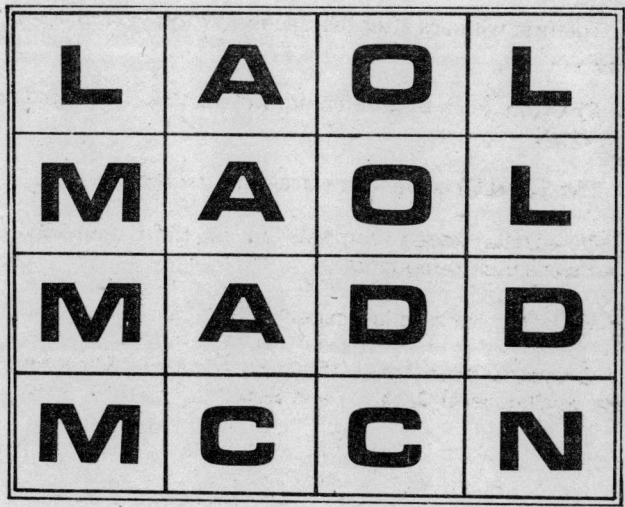

A famous striker who was on the losing side for his club at Wembley in 1978.

INTERNATIONALS

To be selected for one's country is the ultimate for most footballers. Here are some questions about the lucky few who have made the grade.

1 Who holds the record for playing the most consecutive internationals (70) for England?

2 Arsenal once provided the England team with seven players in the same match. Against whom?

3 And in what year? 1914, 1924 or 1934?

4 Name the seven players.

5 When did Ray Clemence make his debut for England?

6 Who won more caps, Dixie Dean or David Jack?

7 Cyril Knowles played for England. True or false?

8 Did Bernard Joy ever play for his country?

9 Martin Peters won how many caps? 47, 67 or 87?

10 How many players by the name of Wilkins have played for England?

This midfield player has been a long-serving captain of Wales. Name him.

K
C
R
E

U
S
N
A

F
P
E
S

Unjumble the letters to find a legendary Hungarian forward of the post-war years.

1 Is it correct that Halifax Town have never had an international player on their books?

2 Who was Fulham's most capped player?

3 How many times did he play for his country?

4 Eddie McCreadie played 10, 23 or 40 times for Scotland?

5 Who was the Scottish international who played for Charlton and spoke with a South African accent?

6 Burnley's most capped player was an Irishman named . . . .

7 How many times did Brian Clough play for England?

8 Roger Byrne was England's most capped right-back. True or false?

9 After making two appearances for England in 1966, a Liverpool player was suddenly recalled by England in 1978. Who was he?

10 How many times has Stan Bowles been selected by England?

1 Ipswich manager Bobby Robson played 20 times for England. Which club was he with at the time?

2 How many times did Terry Venables play for England?

3 Who played more times for his country, Wilf Mannion or Len Shackleton?

4 What have these England internationals in common: Raich Carter, John Atyeo, Eddie Baily, Gerry Hitchens and Stuart Pearson.

5 Alan Ball's last international appearance was in . . .?

6 How many caps did Ball win?

7 Was it true that his father also played for England?

8 The record crowd for an international in Great Britain was 149,547 in 1937. What was the ground?

9 What year did England beat Portugal 10–0?

10 What was the score when the teams met in the 1966 World Cup?

This former England international was the First Division's leading scorer in 1978-9. Who is he?

MANAGERS

Managers are the most important people in the game. They direct how the players play and in most cases, how football clubs are run.

1 When was Bob Paisley appointed manager of Liverpool?

2 Lawrie McMenemy, the Southampton manager, played for which clubs?

3 Ron Saunders has managed . . .?

4 The longest serving of the First Division managers is . . .?

5 Who was the manager who quit football to become an evangelist in America?

6 Who is the First Division manager whose son plays for his club first team?

7 Who is the oldest manager in the Football League?

8 Who succeeded Bill Nicholson as manager of Spurs?

9 Liverpool have only had five managers since the war. True or false?

10 Who was the manager who was involved in a famous High Court case in the 1978–9 season?

Can you recognise this former WBA manager?

This man managed Crystal Palace before Malcolm Allison.

1 Who succeeded Jack Charlton as manager of Middlesbrough?

2 Ronnie Allen has managed two Midlands First Division clubs. Which are they?

3 Who was the manager of the successful Argentina side in the 1978 World Cup?

4 Who was Ron Greenwood's predecessor as manager of West Ham?

5 Who is the Tottenham Hotspur assistant manager?

6 George Eastham once managed . . .?

7 Who was the former English club manager who led New York Cosmos to success in the NASL in 1978?

8 Two famous managers spent just over a month as manager of Leeds. Who were they?

9 Bobby Charlton was manager of which Third Division club?

10 Who was appointed temporary manager of Chelsea when Ken Shellito was fired?

REFEREES

Referees have the most difficult task of anyone connected with football. Whatever decision they make, they are sure to upset someone but without referees there would be no game of football!

1 Who was the referee who booked Johan Cruyff in the 1974 World Cup Final?

2 Name the Welsh referee who took part in the 1978 World Cup Finals.

3 A recently retired referee once played at centre-half for Bolton. He is Bob . . . .

4 Who refereed the World Cup Final between Brazil and Italy in 1970? Rudi . . . .

5 The Englishman who refereed the 1950 World Cup Final later became chairman of an English club. What was his name and which was the club?

6 A former referee became President of FIFA. Name him?

7 Name a country which has full-time professional referees.

8 A FIFA referee who represented Wales announced his retirement near the end of the 1978-9 season. Who was he?

9 The referee who became a Government Minister was . . .?

10 A famous referee who retired in 1978-9 was famous for running backwards. Name him.

This well-known referee appeared in a record number of five matches at Wembley. He is Norman . . . .

FOOTBALL LEAGUE CUP

The League Cup has only been in existence a comparatively short time but is firmly established in the English soccer calendar, especially now the Final is played at Wembley. See if you can answer these questions about it.

1 Who were the first winners in 1960–61?

2 When was the first Final played at Wembley?

3 In 1969, when Third Division Swindon beat Arsenal, who scored two of Swindon's goals?

4 In 1971, another player scored two goals, this time in Tottenham's 2–0 victory over Aston Villa. Who was he?

5 The 1977 Final needed two replays before it was settled. Which team won?

6 Who was the young goalkeeper who played for Nottingham Forest in the 1978 Final?

7 The 1978 Final went to a replay. Who scored the deciding goal?

8 Which team lost the 1979 Final?

9 Who were the losing semi-finalists in 1979?

10 In the Fourth Round, Southampton were held to a 0–0 draw by which Fourth Division club?

This player scored two of Aston Villa's goals in their 3-2
second replay success against Everton in the 1977 League
Cup Final. Who is he?

See if you can identify this Aston Villa player who scored the
only goal of the 1975 Final against Norwich.

1 Which club has appeared in most Finals?

2 Manchester United have never won the League Cup. True or false?

3 Newcastle went down to Manchester City by what score in the 1976 Final?

4 Who were City's goal scorers?

5 Has Malcolm Macdonald ever won a League Cup winner's medal?

6 Have Birmingham City ever won the League Cup?

7 Aldershot once reached the Final when a Fourth Division club. True or false?

8 Has a club ever won the League championship and the League Cup in the same season?

9 How many times have Leeds reached the League Cup Final?

10 A Third Division side known as 'The Seals' reached the semi-final in 1975. Who were they?

EUROPEAN FOOTBALL

Now that foreign players are coming into the Football League, there is an increasing interest in European football. To be an expert these days, fans need to know all about it. See how you fare with these questions.

1 Manchester United were knocked out of the 1977–78 European Cup Winners' Cup in the second round by which club?

2 Two Dutch clubs have won the European Cup four times between them. Name the clubs.

3 Who scored Liverpool's goal in the 1978 European Cup Final against Bruges?

4 The UEFA Cup started in what year?

5 Who were the first winners?

6 What is the biggest stadium in Portugal? The Stadium of . . ., Lisbon.

7 No Spanish club has ever won the UEFA Cup. True or false?

8 Inter Milan won the European Cup in which years?

9 Sweden's entrants in the 1978–79 European Cup were . . .?

10 Who thought up the idea of a European Cup?

He scored a goal on his 19th birthday in the 1978 European Cup Final. Who is he?

This forward played an important part in Southampton's bid to lift the European Cup-Winners' Cup in 1976–77.

1 Italian clubs AC Milan and Inter-Milan play on the same ground. What is it called?

2 Which was the English club that entered the 1955–56 European Cup only to withdraw on the advice of the Football League?

3 The following year another English club disregarded similar advice and reached the semi-final before going out to the eventual winners, Real Madrid. Name the club.

4 How old was Puskas when he made his debut for Real Madrid in 1958. 28, 32 or 35?

5 Glasgow Rangers were beaten 12–4 on aggregate in the semi-final of the 1960 European Cup, by whom?

6 The first club to beat Real Madrid and end their 5-year unbeaten run in the European Cup was . . .?

7 Who was the manager of the Benfica side which won the European Cup twice? Bela G . . . .

8 The first European Cup Final to be held in England was between Benfica and AC Milan in . . .?

9 Who scored Celtic's winning goal in the 1967 European Cup Final?

10 Who were Manchester United's opponents in the 1968 Final?

1 There were two British teams in the 1970 European Cup and they met in the semi-final. Who were they?

2 A goalkeeper called Economopoulos was on the losing side in the 1971 Final played at Wembley. Which club did he play for?

3 Arsenal were knocked out of the 1972 competition by . . .?

4 Leeds lost the 1975 Final in Paris by a score of 2–0 . . . to which German club?

5 The first European Cup Winners' Cup Final was played in . . .?

6 Who scored both West Ham's goals in the 1965 European Cup Winners' Cup Final?

7 Name West Ham's opponents.

8 Chelsea's goals in their European Cup Winners' Cup success in 1971 were scored by . . .?

9 Chelsea's opponents were . . . .

10 In the 1976 Final, West Ham lost 4–2 to . . .?

This young goalkeeper conceded four goals in the 1976 European Cup-Winners' Cup Final. Who is he?

GROUNDS

There are 92 Football League grounds in England and Wales and some of them are among the best known footballing arenas in the world. Test your knowledge about them in these questions.

1 Tranmere Rovers play at . . . .

2 Which club's ground has the biggest capacity, Sheffield United or Sheffield Wednesday?

3 The ground record at Sincil Bank, Lincoln is 23,196, 29,556 or 32,334?

4 Name a First Division ground which is named after another sport.

5 Which ground has a horse racing connection?

6 Which club can hold more fans, Liverpool or Manchester United?

7 White Hart Lane once attracted the attendance of 75,038. True or false.

8 Which London ground bears the same name as a wife of Henry VIII?

9 Brighton's ground is called . . .?

10 Which club has a ground whose name is the same as a Second Division manager?

K E P

M O

A H R

A Third Division ground in the West of the country.

Time for a laugh! These jokes originally appeared in *Roy of the Rovers* weekly. But this time we have cut out some of the lettering. See if you can guess the original wording.

SEASON 1978-79

The 1978-79 season was one of the worst for bad weather in the history of the Football League but the postponed matches were eventually fitted in without too many disruptions. Test your knowledge of some of the exciting games that were played.

1 Ipswich were denied a chance of reaching the F.A. Cup Final for the second successive year when they lost to Liverpool in which round of the Cup?

2 Crystal Palace were knocked out of the League Cup by . . .?

3 A goalkeeper at a First Division club lost his place because he'd eaten too many sweet things. Who was he?

4 Two players of the same side were sent off for fighting in January, 1979. Name them.

5 Name the club that was fined £15,000 by the Football League for illegal payments, including one to George Best?

6 A centre-forward made his debut for a First Division club who is also a heavyweight boxer. Who was he?

7 When the two top players of the year, Osvaldo Ardiles and Liam Brady came up against each other at White Hart Lane in a League match, whose side won and by how many?

8 Chelsea signed a Yugoslav international goalkeeper Petar Borota. What was his previous club?

9 The first club to take over from Liverpool at the top of the First Division was . . .?

10 Which club signed Charlie George from Derby?

Can you identify this member of Liverpool's successful side in 1978–79?

Manchester United tried this player as a striker in one match but he was soon back to his usual position. Who is he?

1 Who was the London centre-half who joined Derby for £275,000?

2 Arsenal eventually beat Sheffield Wednesday in the F.A. Cup after how many matches?

3 Arnold Muhren, the Ipswich midfield player, was signed from . . .?

4 Who became the manager of QPR in succession to Frank Sibley? And who succeeded Sibley's successor?

5 Who was the first coloured player to represent England?

6 Who was the Polish World Cup star who signed for Manchester City?

7 Fulham nearly signed an ex-Brazilian World Cup star. What was his name?

8 Ipswich had one of its best players sent off in a European Cup Winners' Cup tie at Innsbruck. Who was he?

9 Which caretaker manager almost took Sunderland to promotion and was then not given the job?

10 England beat Northern Ireland in a European Championship match by what score?

1 Sir Alf Ramsey was invited to the Middle East to discuss a possible job. Name the country.

2 The transfer fee paid for Phil Parkes by West Ham, which set a record for a goalkeeper, was £500,000, £565,000 or £580,000?

3 Newcastle signed a player from a non-League club for £10,000 and he was an instant success. Who was he?

4 Who was the player who joined Manchester City from Plymouth at the second attempt?

5 Peter Ward lost his place in the Brighton side for a time to . . .?

6 Name the record signing who stayed on the bench for most of his early matches with a successful Midlands club.

7 Alex Stepney left Manchester United after 13 years and joined American club . . . .

8 Chelsea signed one of their former stars from Philadelphia Fury. Name him.

9 Britain's most expensive centre-half was dropped by Scotland. Who was he?

10 Who was the man appointed manager of the England Youth team?

This player made a comeback as a defender after playing all
his career in midfield. Can you identify him?

Trevor Francis became Britain's first £1m footballer when Nottingham Forest bought him from Birmingham City. Overnight he became one of the game's leading personalities and to find out how much you know about this brilliant young footballer, here are some questions about him.

1 Where was Trevor born?

2 Whom did he make his Nottingham Forest debut against? ·

3 His first club was . . .?

4 In season 1977–78, he was Birmingham's leading scorer with 20, 25 or 30 goals?

5 He played in how many of Birmingham's League matches that season – 32, 40 or 42?

6 What number shirt did he wear?

7 How tall is Trevor?

8 And what is his weight?

9 Trevor has scored, on average, one goal every three, four or five matches?

10 What is his wife's name?

N

L

S

A

U

C

S

I

L

T

Re-arrange these letters and you will find the name of the manager who signed Trevor as a fifteen-year-old!

SPOT THE DIFFERENCE

On this and the next five pages you will find some illustrations from recent issues of *Roy of the Rovers*. At first glance, each pair of pictures may look alike . . . but our artist has made six changes to one of each pair of pictures. See if you can spot the differences.

HAT TRICKS

The ambition of every striker is to score a hat trick but not all achieve it. Here are some posers about some of the players who have scored three or more goals in a single game.

1 Who is the only player to score a hat trick in the Final of a World Cup competition?

2 Has Eddie Gray of Leeds ever scored a hat trick?

3 When Ipswich put Millwall out of the F.A. Cup on March 11th, 1978 which of their players scored three times?

4 When Spurs beat Bristol Rovers on October 22nd, 1977 two players scored hat tricks. Who were they?

5 A WBA player once scored three hat tricks in eight days in September, 1965. Name him.

6 Two players have scored four goals in five minutes. True or false?

7 Denis Law once scored a double hat trick in an abandoned F.A. Cup tie in 1961. Who were Manchester City's opponents?

8 Ted MacDougall once scored two hat tricks in a fortnight in 1975–76. What club was he playing for?

9 A Tranmere Rovers player scored four hat tricks in the 1975–76 season. He was Ron . . . .

10 Has Malcolm Macdonald ever scored a hat trick for England?

Can you recognise this Scottish hat trick hero?

FOOTBALL FIRSTS

There has to be a first time for every feat in football. It's interesting to recall moments when history was made. Can you remember these 'firsts'?

1 The first England v Scotland game was played at a cricket ground . . . in what year?

2 England's first defeat in international football by a foreign team was in 1929 . . . Against whom?

3 England's first home defeat by an overseas team was in 1953 at the hands of . . . ?

4 Who was the first player to win England honours at five levels, schoolboy, Youth, Amateur, Under-23 and Senior?

5 The first Football League game under lights was at Portsmouth in 1956, 1959 or 1960?

6 When were shinguards first used?

7 The first substitute used in a League game was Charlton's long-serving captain in 1965. Name him.

8 The first £1,000 player to be transferred was . . .?

9 And the first £100,000 player?

10 The first club to win the F.A. Cup this century was . . . ?

H I L W

G T L

R Y B I

Rejig these letters and you will discover the name of the first England player to gain 100 caps.

HERE AND THERE

1 Name the six men who have played in and managed Football League Championship winning teams.

2 The smallest number of players called on by a club when winning the League championship was fourteen by . . . in 1965–66.

3 Who scored the fastest goal in League football?

4 How long after the start did he score it?

5 Which was the West Country team that once went 58 matches without using a substitute?

6 Who was the tallest player ever to play in a League match?

7 And the shortest?

8 The First Division record for the fewest goals against in a season is held by . . . in season 1978-79.

9 Fewest goals scored by a club in Division One came in the 1977-78 season. Name the club.

10 The highest score in a World Cup match was a 12–0 victory by West Germany over . . .?

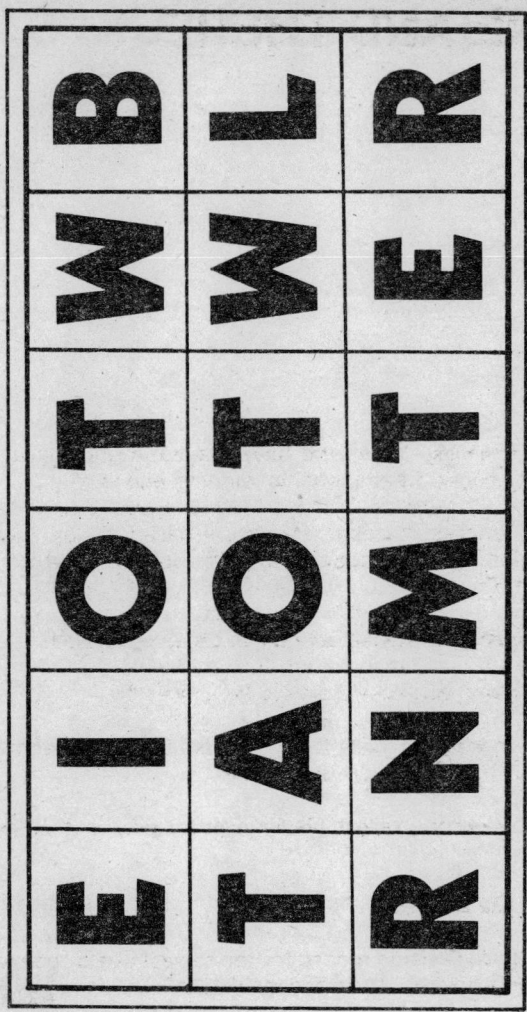

The first England football team manager. But the letters are all mixed-up.

INTERNATIONAL CAPS

1 Which of these England right backs gained most caps. Jimmy Armfield or Alf Ramsey?

2 The goalkeeper with the highest number of caps for England is . . .?

3 Who is Scotland's most capped player?

4 A Swedish international overtook Bobby Moore's world record of 108 caps in the 1978 World Cup. What is his name?

5 The youngest player ever to be picked by England at the age of 18 years 183 days was . . .?

6 Have any players appeared for more than one country in the Home Championship?

7 A Blackburn Rovers wing-half played 35 times for England in the Fifties. Name him.

8 Nobby Stiles played 19, 28 or 35 times for England?

9 Has Alfie Conn ever played for Scotland?

10 Before going on to earn more caps for Scotland while with Spurs, goalkeeper Bill Brown was capped at another club. Name it.

Who is the Welsh striker who scored a hat trick against Scotland in 1979?

TRUE OR FALSE?

All you have to do is say if the following statements are true or false.

1 A man named Wedlock once played for England.

2 Frank Stapleton was born in Belfast.

3 Frank O'Farrell was once manager of the Iran national side.

4 Paddy Mulligan is one of the most capped players in the history of Eire football.

5 Kevin Lock of Fulham never played for the England Under-23 side.

6 When he appeared in this year's League Cup Final, Gary Birtles had only played for one professional club, Nottingham Forest.

7 Millwall have never played in the First Division.

8 Mansfield Town are known as The Stags.

9 Leicester City's top scorer in the 1977–78 season scored only four goals.

10 Ipswich have only had five managers since the war.

This former Scottish international once played for Southampton. True or false?

Before joining Leeds, this Welsh international was with Burnley. True or false?

1 Dave Swindlehurst (Crystal Palace) came on as a substitute for England during the 1979 summer tour.

2 Before joining Coventry City, Ian Wallace was with Glasgow Rangers.

3 Crewe Alexandra are known as The Railwaymen.

4 Chelsea have a female secretary.

5 An ex-Millwall manager is secretary of Charlton.

6 Northampton have never been in the First Division.

7 Cardiff City were once known as Riverside F.C.

8 Bury are known as The Shakers.

9 Burnley were original members of the Football League.

10 Ron Greenwood was born in Brighton.

DATES

Some people can remember dates, others find it very hard. How good are you on these dates?

1 Norwich City reached the semi-final of the F.A. Cup as a Third Division side in which year?

2 In which year were Nottingham Forest promoted from the Second Division?

3 Orient were in the First Division in what season?

4 Wimbledon were elected to the Football League in . . .?

5 West Ham were formed in which year?

6 The World Cup championship was started in . . .?

7 Arsenal won the EUFA Cup in what year?

8 The first winners of the European Football championship for countries was in the USSR in . . .?

9 Bobby Charlton first played for England in what year?

10 When did Fulham last play in the First Division?

This famous manager took charge of Leeds United in what year?

Chelsea's record signing David Hay cost £225,000 when he joined them from Celtic in which year?

1 Martin Peters left West Ham to join Spurs in which year?

2 Tottenham have been promoted back to the First Division on two occasions in their first season in the Second Division. In what years?

3 When were Arsenal last in the Second Division?

4 Celtic won every competition open to them in . . .?

5 Spurs and Scotland forward John White was fatally struck by lightning in which year?

6 Bryan Robson was the Football League's top scorer. When?

7 Liverpool won the League championship and the European Cup in what year?

8 Portsmouth won the League championship in successive years in . . .?

9 When was the League extended from 88 to 92 clubs?

10 The oldest League club, Notts County, was formed in . . .?

LAWS

Very few people read the laws of the game, even the professional players. But the laws are an essential part of F.A. Coaching courses and if you want to qualify as a coach, you must first pass a test on the laws. These questions will aid your knowledge.

1 What is the maximum length of a football pitch?

2 What is the minimum width?

3 Is it compulsory to have a flag staff on the halfway line?

4 What is the width of the lines?

5 Can play continue if the crossbar breaks and a new one fitted?

6 Do goal posts have to be round, square or any particular shape?

7 Can the post be made of metal?

8 Are goal nets compulsory?

9 Does the ball have to be a particular colour?

10 Can a substitute come on anywhere else but the halfway line?

1 A player who is about to be substituted refuses to take any notice of the manager who is calling him off. Is the referee entitled to stop the game and tell him to go off?

2 Is it necessary for players to wear boots?

3 If the referee decides to give the advantage to the team in possession, after a foul has been committed against one of its players, can he later blow up and award the free-kick when possession is lost?

4 What is the laid down time for the interval?

5 Is it possible to score straight from the kick off?

6 If the ball is two-thirds the way over the line, is it out of play?

7 A defender's clearance hits the referee and rebounds into goal. Does it count as a goal?

8 Can a player be offside when the referee drops the ball?

9 How many offences qualify for the award of a direct free-kick?

10 What is the punishment for dangerous play?

1 What action should the referee take if two players of the same side come to blows with each other?

2 Does a free kick have to be taken from the exact spot where an offence has taken place?

3 Is it possible for defenders to be within ten yards of a free kick?

4 A defender takes a free kick outside the penalty area and passes back to his goalkeeper. But the goalkeeper isn't looking and the ball goes into the net. What decision does the referee come to?

5 After the referee has signalled for a the kick to be taken at a penalty, a colleague of the penalty taker encroaches into the penalty area. The penalty is converted. What action should the referee take?

6 The kicker takes a penalty and the ball rebounds to him off a post and he scores from his second shot. Does the goal count?

7 Can a goalkeeper take a throw in?

8 A corner kick is taken and the ball rebounds to the taker off the referee. He centres and the ball goes into the goal. Is it a goal?

9 Is it possible to score direct from a corner?

10 What is the punishment for violent conduct?

1 Can the referee stop a player wearing a medallion around his neck.

2 Can a manager or coach shout advice from the touchline?

3 Does a referee add injury time on at the end of the first half if injuries occur in the first half, or at the end of the game? ·

4 Can a referee alter a decision?

5 Is it permissible for a forward to remove the corner flag when taking a corner?

6 Can a player by offside in his own half of the field?

7 Is it possible to be offside direct from a goal kick?

8 A defender deliberately brings an opponent down inside the area but the ball is running out of play and there is no danger of a goal resulting. What decision does the referee give?

9 A player uses abusive language to the referee as the teams are coming out. Is the referee justified in showing him the red card?

10 The trainer comes on without permission of the referee to treat a player. What does the referee do?

ANSWERS

FIRST DIVISION Section, pages 8-11

Page 8
1. 1888. 2. Preston North End. 3. Middlesbrough. 4. 1936/7. 5. None. 6. Nottingham Forest. 7. Derby County. 8. West Ham, Newcastle and Leicester. 9. Norwich City and John Bond. 10. Derby County.

Page 9
Chelsea.

Page 10
Bolton.

Page 11
1. Sunderland. 2. Wolves. 3. Twice. 4. Brian Clough. 5. Portman Road. 6. Dave Mackay and Tommy Docherty. 7. 1967. 8. Danny Blanchflower. 9. 1974-75. 10. Brunton Park.

SECOND DIVISION Section, pages 12 and 13

Page 12
1. 1948-49. 2. Crystal Palace. 3. No. 4. latics. 5. Alex Sabella of Sheffield United. 6. Millwall. 7. Bobby Moore. 8. 1972. 9. Manchester United. 10. Duncan McKenzie.

Page 13
Sheffield United.

THIRD DIVISION Section, pages 14 and 15

Page 14
Rotherham United.

Page 15
1. 1967. 2. Bury. 3. Ron Atkinson. 4. No. 5. Bolton. 6. Pat Earles. 7. Priestfield Stadium. 8. Brentford. 9. Blue shirts with white stripes. 10. The Owls.

FOURTH DIVISION Section, pages 16 and 17

Page 16
1. Rochdale. 2. True. 3. Hartlepool. 4. Southport. 5. Ron and Graham Atkinson. 6. 1958. 7. Graham Taylor. 8. Stockport County. 9. Peterborough. 10. True.

Page 17
Wigan Athletic.

SCOTLAND Section, pages 18–21

Page 18
1. Bobby Collins. 2. Three times. 3. Liverpool. 4. True. 5. Billy Steel. 6. Falkirk. 7. George Young. 8. James McGrory. 9. John Greig. 10. Yes.

Page 19
Kenny Dalglish.

Page 20
The Scotland team that lost 3–1 to Peru in the 1978 World Cup in Argentina.

Page 21
1. Because Willie Johnston failed a drugs test. 2. Torino. 3. Austria. 4. £116,000. 5. Hughie Gallacher. 6. 1–1. 7. Denis Law. 8. Aberdeen. 9. East Stirling. 10. Yes.

WALES Section, pages 22 and 23

Page 22
1. Trevor Ford. 2. Ivor Allchurch. 3. True. 4. 22. 5. Arfon Griffiths. 6. 1927. 7. Bluebirds. 8. No. 9. 1937. 10. Billy Meredith.

Page 23
Shrewsbury Town.

NORTHERN IRELAND Section, pages 24 and 25

Page 24
1. 1964. 2. Billy Bingham. 3. Dave Clements. 4. Chris Nicholl. 5. Shrewsbury, Swansea City and Crewe Alexandra. 6. England. 7. Terry Neill. 8. Belfast. 9. Bob Latchford. 10. Ards.

Page 25
Carrick Rangers.

WORLD CUP Section, pages 26-31

Page 26
1. Mario Kempes. 2. 6. 3. Torocsik and Nyilasi of Hungary and Nanninga of Holland. 4. Brazil. 5. 12. 6. Nanninga. 7. S. Gonella (Italy). 8. Bernard Lacombe (France). 9. Brazil 2, Italy 1. 10. Leao.

Page 27
Cubillas (Peru) and Dirceu (Brazil).

Page 28
South America 6, Europe 5.

Page 29
1. Alan Rough, Bobby Clark, Jim Blyth. 2. Kenny Burns, Archie Gemmill, John Robertson. 3. West Germany's. 4. West Germany again. 5. Hurucan. 6. Ernst Happel. 7. Ronnie Hellstrom. 8. Bastia. 9. Joe Jordan. 10. Ernie Brandts.

Page 30
18.

Page 31
1. Brazil. 2. Gerd Müller. 3. Johan Neeskens. 4. Portugal 2, USSR 1. 5. Martin Peters. 6. 1–1. 7. Eusebio. 8. 1954. 9. Four times. 10. Farmer.

KEVIN KEEGAN Section, pages 32 and 33

Page 32
1. Hans Krankl. 2. Mighty Mouse. 3. Armthorpe. 4. Scunthorpe. 5. 7. 6. June, 1977. 7. £500,000. 8. £440,000. 9. Wales. 10. 1973.

Page 33
1. Trevor Francis. 2. Brazil. 3. 21. 4. 1971. 5. £35,000. 6. Andy Beattie. 7. Bill Shankly. 8. Two. 9. Berti Vogts. 10. Phil Neal.

WINGERS, pages 34–39

Page 34
1. Tom Finney. 2. Finney. 3. Bryan Douglas. 4. Billy Bingham. 5. Steve Coppell and Gordon Hill. 6. Glasgow Rangers. 7. Southend and Crystal Palace. 8. Norwich. 9. Burnley. 10. Nigeria.

Page 35
Gordon Hill.

Page 36
Clive Woods.

Page 37
1. Dublin. 2. Ken Barnes. 3. Tranmere. 4. Rene Houseman. 5. Clive Walker. 6. Terry Curran and Gerry Ryan. 7. Peter Marinello. 8. Carl Harris and Arthur Graham. 9. Terry Paine. 10. Cliff Bastin.

Page 38
1. One. 2. 1931. 3. 35. 4. 1965. 5. Malta. 6. 1954. 7. Billy Meredith. 8. Cliff Bastin. 9. Cliff Jones, Terry Medwin, Terry Dyson. 10. Alan Morton.

Page 39
Francisco Gento.

DEFENDERS, pages 40–45

Page 40
1. Tommy Taylor. 2. Manny Andruszewski. 3. Larry Lloyd, Viv Anderson, Kenny Burns. 4. Blackpool and Stockport County. 5. Kevin Hird. 6. Highbury. 7. Aston Villa. 8. George Best. 9. Mark Higgins. 10. True.

Page 41
Frank McLintock.

Page 42
Mick Mills.

Page 43
1. Tommy Booth. 2. Martin Buchan. 3. Barnsley. 4. Glen Roeder. 5. False. 6. George Berry and Bob Hazell. 7 Swansea City, Northampton Town, Arsenal and Birmingham City. 8. Norman Hunter. 9. 1973 against Yugoslavia. 10 Willie Donachie.

Page 44
1. Scotland. 2. 105. 3. Everton. 4. Southampton and Spurs. 5. 27.
6. Bobby Charltcn. 7. Ray Wilson. 8. Barking. 9. Jack Charlton.
10. John Charles.

Page 45
Ron Yeats.

F.A. CUP, pages 46-51

Page 46
1. Newcastle and Arsenal have won five each. 2. Six. 3. 1939. Yes,
they won it once. 5. Four times each. 6. Ipswich. 7. Ian Porterfield.
8. Exhaustion. 9. Bert Trautmann. 10. No.

Page 47
Stuart Pearson.

Page 48
Charlie George.

Page 49
1. Yes, but an F.A. official is in front of them. 2. True. 3. Yeovil. 4.
George Mutch. 5. The Queen. 6. Eddie McCreadie. 7. David Jack.
8. Mike Trebilcock. 9. Orient and WBA. 10. Everton.

Page 50
1. 1872. 2. The Oval. 3. 1923. 4. Wanderers. 5. Derby County. 6.
Burnley. 7. False. 8. Blackpool and Arsenal. 9. Joe Harvey. 10
Jack Fairbrother and Ron Simpson.

Page 51
Malcolm Macdonald.

INTERNATIONALS, pages 52-57

Page 52
1. Billy Wright. 2. Italy. 3. 1934. 4. Frank Moss, George Male,
Eddie Hapgood, Wilf Copping, Raymond Bowden, Ted Drake and
Cliff Bastin. 5. 1973. 6. Dixie Dean. 7. True. 8. Yes, once. 9. 67.
10. One.

Page 53
Terry Yorath.

Page 54
Ferenc Puskas.

Page 55
1. Yes it is correct. 2. Johnny Haynes. 3. 56. 4. 23. 5. John Hewie.
6. Jimmy McIlroy. 7. Twice. 8. False. 9. Ian Callaghan. 10. 5 times.

Page 56
1. WBA. 2. 2. 3. Wilf Mannion. 4. They each scored 5 goals for
England. 5. 1975. 6. 72. 7. No. 8. Hampden Park. 9. 1947. 10.
2-1.

Page 57
Frank Worthington.

MANAGERS, Pages 58-61

Page 58
1. 1974. 2. Newcastle United, Gateshead. 3. Yeovil, Oxford,
Norwich, Manchester City and Aston Villa. 4. Alan Dicks, Bristol
City. 5. Willie Bell. 6. John Bond. 7. Alec Stock, Bournemouth. 8.
Terry Neill. 9. True. 10. Tommy Docherty.

Page 59
Johnny Giles.

Page 60
Bert Head.

Page 61
1. John Neal. 2. Wolves and WBA. 3. Cesar Menotti. 4. Ted
Fenton. 5. Pat Welton. 6. Stoke City. 7. Eddie Firmani. 8. Brian
Clough and Jock Stein. 9. Preston North End. 10. Frank Upton.

REFEREES, pages 62-63

Page 62
1. Jack Taylor. 2. Clive Thomas. 3. Bob Matthewson. 4. Rudi
Glockner. 5. George Reader (Southampton). 6. Sir Stanley Rous.
7. Brazil. 8. Tom Reynolds. 9. Denis Howell. 10. Roger Kirkpatrick.

Page 63
Norman Burtenshaw.

THE FOOTBALL LEAGUE CUP, pages 64-67

Page 64
1. Aston Villa. 2. 1967. 3. Don rogers. 4. Martin Chivers. 5. Aston Villa. 6. Chris Woods. 7. John Robertson. 8. Southampton. 9. Leeds and Watford. 10. Reading.

Page 65
Brian Little.

Page 66
Ray Graydon.

Page 67
1. Aston Villa. 2. True. 3. 2-1. 4. Barnes and Tueart. 5. No. 6. Yes. 7. False. 8. Yes, Nottingham Forest, 1978. 9. Once. 10. Chester.

EUROPEAN FOOTBALL pages 68-73

Page 68
1. Porto. 2. Feyenoord and Ajax. 3. Kenny Dalglish. 4. 1972. 5. Tottenham Hotspur. 6. Stadium of Light, Lisbon. 7. True. 8. 1964 and 1965. 9. Malmo FF. 10. Gilbert Hanot, a French journalist.

Page 69
Brian Kidd.

Page 70
Mike Channon.

Page 71
1. San Siro. 2. Chelsea. 3. Manchester United. 4. 32. 5. Eintracht Frankfurt. 6. Barcelona. 7. Bela Guttman. 8. 1963. 9. Steve Chalmers. 10. Benfica.

Page 72
1. Leeds and Celtic. 2. Panathinaikos. 3. Ajax. 4. Bayern Munich. 5. 1961. 6. Alan Sealey. 7. TSV Munich. 8. Osgood and Dempsey. 9. Real Madrid. 10. Anderlecht.

Page 73
Mervyn Day.

GROUNDS, pages 74–75

Page 74

1. Prenton Park. 2. Sheffield Wednesday. 3. 23,196. 4. The Baseball Ground, Derby. 5. The Racecourse ground, Wrexham. 6. Manchester United. 7. True. 8. The Boleyn Ground, West Ham. 9. The Goldstone Ground. 10. Blackpool (Bloomfield Road).

Page 75

Home Park, Plymouth.

JOKE SECTION, pages 76–81

These are the original captions:

Page 76

I'm getting . . . warmed up for the match.
. . . He's our new striker!

Page 77

It's a spot the ball competition!
No! Brian Clough is . . . satisfied with Peter Shilton!

Page 78

A hundred and thirty four times. Why?
"I reckon I might have scored if . . . you hadn't fouled the ref!"

Page 79

Explains that bit of magic when you . . . dribbled round seven of their players!
. . . I don't think it's a fair game!

Page 80

"I reckon he thinks I'm a zebra crossing, Ref . . . He keeps walking over me!"
"I'm . . . playing on the wing!"

Page 81

Cold Trafford and Stamford Fridge!
That was a high-spirited . . . GHOUL!

SEASON 1978-79, pages 82-87

Page 82
1. Sixth Round. 2. Aston Villa. 3. Mark Kendall (Spurs). 4. Derek Hales and Mike Flanagan. 5. Fulham. 6. Justin Fashanau (Norwich City). 7. Arsenal 5-0. 8. Partisan Belgrade. 9. WBA. 10. Southampton.

Page 83
Phil Thompson (Liverpool).

Page 84
Lou Macari

Page 85
1. Steve Wicks. 2. Five. 3. Twente enschede. 4. Steve Burtenshaw, followed by Tommy Docherty. 5. Viv Anderson. 6. Kazimierz Deyne. 7. Paulo Cesar. 8. Paul Mariner. 9. Billy elliott. 10. 4-0.

Page 86
1. Kuwait. 2. £565,000. 3. Alan Shoulder. 4. Barry Silkman. 5. Malcolm Poskett. 6. David Mills. 7. Dallas Tornado. 8. Peter Osgood. 9. Gordon McQueen. 10. John Cartwright.

Page 87
Colin Bell.

TREVOR FRANCIS, pages 88-89

Page 88
1. Plymouth. 2. Ipswich. 3. Birmingham City. 4. 25. 5. 42. 6. 8. 7. Five feet ten inches. 8. Eleven stone, seven pounds. 9. One goal in three. 10. Helen.

Page 89
Stan Cullis.

SPOT THE DIFFERENCE Section, pages 90-95

Pages 91-92
One floodlight missing. Finger from goalie's right hand missing. Line from the football missing. Section of the crowd behind goal net missing. Lines on goalie's right boot missing. Apostrophe missing from the word "It's".

Pages 92-93
Arm missing from the background player in white. Shadow missing from beneath player who has fallen. Bottom right-hand side of picture, player's arm band missing. Sock on right leg of referee missing. In crowd section, the first banner is missing. Hyphen missing from "Free-kick".

Pages 94-95
Letter 'O' missing from exclamation 'OOO-OOOPS!'. On left-hand side of picture, above flag, banner missing. On player in dark clothes, shadow missing from left leg. Letter 'B' missing from advertising sign. Side-burn missing from player in dark clothes. Studs missing from right shoe of player in dark clothes.

HAT-TRICKS, pages 96-97

Page 96
1. Geoff Hurst. 2. Yes. 3. Paul Mariner. 4. Ian Moores, Colin Lee. 5. Jeff Astle. 6. True. 7. Luton. 8. Norwich City. 9. Ron Moore. 10. Yes.

Page 97
Willie Pettigrew.

FOOTBALL FIRSTS, pages 98-99

Page 98
1. 1872. 2. Spain. 3. Hungary. 4. Terry Venables. 5. 1956. 6. 1874. 7. Keith Peacock. 8. Alf Common. 9. Denis Law. 10. Bury.

Page 99
Billy Wright.

HERE AND THERE, pages 100-101

Page 100
1. Ted Drake, Bill Nicholson, Alf Ramsey, Joe Mercer, Dave Mackay, Bob Paisley. 2. Liverpool. 3. Jim Fryatt. 4. Four seconds. 5. Bristol City. 6. Albert Iremonger. 7. Fred le May. 8. Liverpool. 9. Leicester. 10. Cyprus.

Page 101
Walter Winterbottom.

INTERNATIONAL CAPS, pages 102-103

Page 102
1. Jimmy Armfield. 2. Gordon Banks. 3. Kenny Dalglish. 4. Bjorn Nordqvist. 5. Duncan Edwards. 6. Yes. 7. Ron Clayton. 8. 28. 9. Yes. 10. Dundee.

Page 103
John Toshack.

TRUE OR FALSE, pages 104-107

Page 104
1. True. 2. False. 3. True. 4. True. 5. False. 6. True. 7. True. 8. True. 9. True. 10. True.

Page 105
George Graham (false).

Page 106
Brian Flynn (true).

Page 107
1. False. 2. False. 3. True. 4. True. 5. True. 6. False. 7. True. 8. True. 9. True. 10. False.

DATES, pages 108–111

Page 108
1. 1959. 2. 1976-77. 3. 1962-63. 4. 1977. 5. 1900. 6. 1930.
7. 1970. 8. 1960. 9. 1958. 10. 1968.

Page 109
Jimmy Adamson 1978.

Page 110
David Hay 1974

Page 111
1. 1970. 2. 1919–20, 1977–78. 3. 1919. 4. 1908 and 1967. 5.
1964. 6. 1972-73. 7. 1976–77. 8. 1948–49, 1949–50. 9.
1950. 10. 1862.

LAWS, pages 112–115

Page 112
1. 130 yards. 2. 50. 3. No. 4. Five inches. 5. Yes. 6. No particular
shape. 7. Yes. 8. No. 9. No. 10. No.

Page 113
1. No. 2. No. 3. No. 4. Five minutes. 5. No. 6. No. 7. Yes. 8. No. 9.
Nine. 10. An indirect free-kick.

Page 114
1. Send both players off. 2. Yes, except when the offence is in the
goal area. 3. Yes, when an indirect free-kick is awarded within ten
yards of the goal line. 4. A corner. 5. Caution the encroacher and
order the kick to be retaken. 6. No. 7. Yes. 8. No, an indirect free
kick to the other team at the point where the taker kicked the ball
the second time. 9. Yes. 10. Expulsion from the field.

Page 115
1. Yes if he thinks it is a danger to other players. 2. No. 3. At the
end of the first half. 4. Yes. 5. No. 6. No. 7. No. 8. Penalty. 9. Yes.
10. Caution the trainer.